I Am Honest

by Jay Dale

Look at me!

I am jumping.

I jump in the mud.

Oh no!

The mud is on the floor.

3

I go to my dad.

5

Look at me!

I am eating.

I eat cereal.

Oh no!

The cereal is on the floor.

I go to my dad.

Look at me!

I am running in the house.

I run into a pot.

Oh no!

The pot is on the floor.

I go to my dad.

13

Look at my dad.

Here is a little cake.

Oh no!

The little cake

is on the floor.

My dad goes
to me!